# Let's Explore
# Science

by Joe Levit

LERNER PUBLICATIONS ◆ MINNEAPOLIS

**Note to Educators**

Throughout this book, you'll find critical-thinking questions. These can be used to engage young readers in thinking critically about the topic and in using the text and photos to do so.

Lerner Publications Company
A division of Lerner Publishing Group, Inc.
241 First Avenue North
Minneapolis, MN 55401 USA

For reading levels and more information, look up this title at www.lernerbooks.com.

**Library of Congress Cataloging-in-Publication Data**

Names: Levit, Joseph, author.
Title: Let's explore science / by Joe Levit.
Description: Minneapolis, MN : Lerner Publications, [2018] | Series: Bumba books—A first look at STEM | Audience: Ages 4–7. | Audience: K to grade 3. | Includes bibliographical references and index.
Identifiers: LCCN 2017046229 (print) | LCCN 2017051667 (ebook) | ISB 9781541507838 (eb pdf) | ISBN 9781541503250 (lb : alk. paper) | ISBN 9781541527010 (pb : alk. paper)
Subjects: LCSH: Science—Juvenile literature. | Scientists—Juvenile literature.
Classification: LCC Q163 (ebook) | LCC Q163 .L4345 2018 (print) | DDC 500—dc23

LC record available at https://lccn.loc.gov/2017046229

Manufactured in the United States of America
1-43820-33653-11/22/2017

# Table of Contents

# What Is Science?

*Science* means "to know."

Some people study the

world to learn more about it.

They are scientists.

Studying science means

asking questions.

Look at the world around you.

You might ask why turtles

have shells.

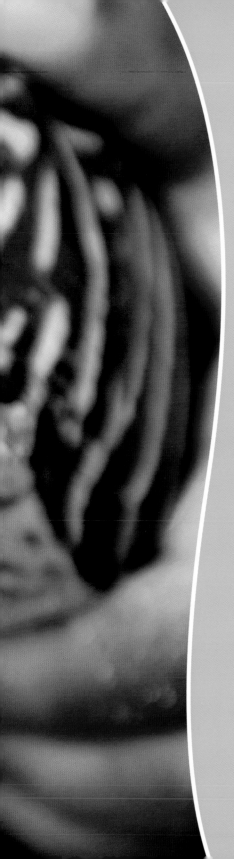

Think about your question. Now guess what the answer might be.

Why do you think turtles have shells?

Then watch what happens.

Gather information about your question.

Check if you were right.

**Shells protect turtles from danger.**

Scientists ask many questions.

They want to find out about the world.

There are many kinds of scientists.

Some scientists study dinosaurs.

They ask questions about what

dinosaurs looked like.

They try to find out what dinosaurs ate.

**How might scientists find out what dinosaurs looked like?**

Some scientists study outer space.

They look through telescopes.

They ask questions about the

planets and stars.

Other scientists study the weather.

They look at data to see when it will rain or be sunny.

What questions do you think weather scientists ask?

You can be a scientist too.

Ask questions about your world.

Then find the answers!

# Science Tools

These are some tools different scientists use.

What other tools might they use?

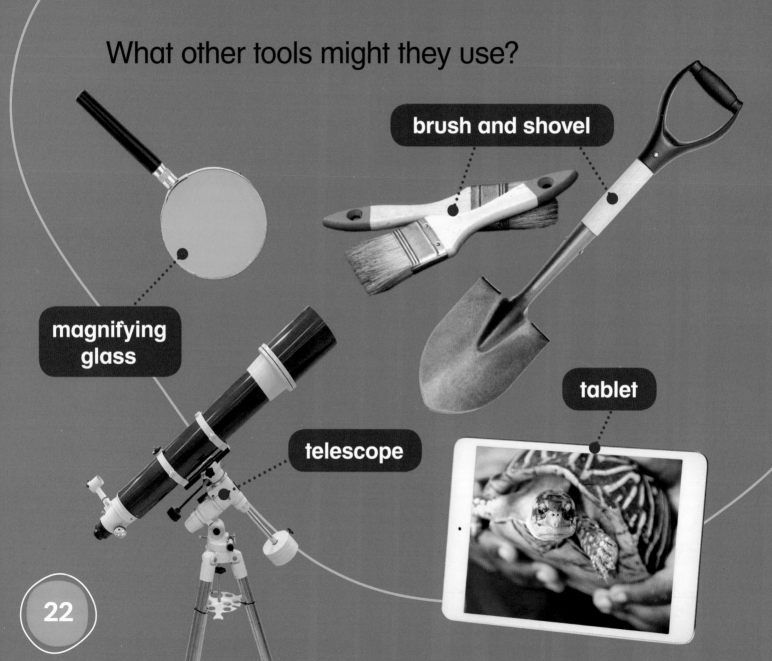

brush and shovel

magnifying glass

telescope

tablet

# Picture Glossary

**data**

facts about something

**scientist**

a person who studies the world

**study**

pay close attention to

**telescope**

a tool used to see things in outer space

# Read More

Dotlich, Rebecca Kai. *What Is Science?* New York: Square Fish, 2016.

Hicks, Kelli L. *I Use Science Tools.* Vero Beach, FL: Rourke, 2012.

Moon, Walt K. *Let's Explore the Stars.* Minneapolis: Lerner Publications, 2018.

# Index

## Photo Credits

The images in this book are used with the permission of: icons: © Amy Salveson/Independent Picture Service; ProStockStudio/Shutterstock.com, p. 5; pyrozhenka/Shutterstock.com, p. 6; Andi Berger/Shutterstock.com, pp. 8–9, 22 (bottom right inset); Jonas Pfister/Shutterstock.com, p. 11; wavebreakmedia/Shutterstock.com, p. 12; ANURAK PONGPATIMET/Shutterstock.com, p. 14; Vadim Sadovski/Shutterstock.com, p. 17; Fineart1/Shutterstock.com, pp. 18–19; Beata Becla/Shutterstock.com, p. 20; BLACKDAY/Shutterstock.com, p. 22 (bottom right); Sergiy1975/Shutterstock.com, p. 22 (bottom left); Vadym Zaitsev/Shutterstock.com, p. 22 (top right); Masarik/Shutterstock.com, p. 22 (top middle); azure1/Shutterstock.com, p. 22 (top left); kdshutterman/Shutterstock.com, p. 23 (top left); Sergey Novikov/Shutterstock.com, p. 23 (top right); mangpor2004/Shutterstock.com, p. 23 (bottom left); Sandratsky Dmitriy/Shutterstock.com, p. 23 (bottom right).

Front cover: wavebreakmedia/Shutterstock.com.